The Life Of Riley
December, 2000 to February 4th, 2015

By

Riley

As Told To

Larry L. Deibert

This is Riley not too long after Peggy and Sean brought him home from the pet store.

This is a true story, but I have taken the liberty of writing it from Riley's point of view.

Larry's Notes

I always wished Riley could talk, because I had many one-sided conversations with him. When I would get my breakfast and lunch ready, he would always be by my feet in the kitchen, probably hoping that I'd give him something to eat, which I usually did. I'd tell him about what I was going to do that day, and he'd cock his head one way and then the other, seemingly expressing great interest in what I was saying.

Prior to that conversation, I'd take him out so he could relieve himself after a nice long sleep, although for me it wasn't always long, because I have always been an early riser. Riley would hop in bed between us, sometimes under the covers lying next to me and he would sleep while Peggy and I watched TV. Of course, most nights I had to get up and take him out before we went to sleep or there would be a good chance he would wake us in the middle of the night.

I'd finish making my lunch and then I'd grab a cup of coffee and whatever I was having for breakfast and head into the living room. I'd sit in my chair, turn on the computer and the TV and Ri would stand in front of me, staring in my eyes and then looking at my toast, bagel, donut or whatever I was eating. I would have to explain that this was my breakfast and point out to him that he had a full bowl of dog food and fresh water for his breakfast and to graze on all day.

Sometimes Peggy would wake up and hear me talking to Riley and I imagine she was shaking her head, thinking me a little crazy. I guess to be a writer, one has to be a little left of center. One morning she actually asked who I was talking to and I said, "I'm talking to Riley." I think I heard her laugh.

So the thought came to me that it would be pretty cool if I would write this book using the words I think Riley would say for certain situations, and I hope I have done him justice.

At the end of this book, Peggy and Sean will share their thoughts about Riley.

This is one of my favorite pictures of Riley. I was lying in bed watching TV and he stood in the doorway long enough for me to take his picture. I think he was about ten.

Meeting Larry
June 2002

1

My name is Riley and I am a dog. I imagine you already knew that by taking a look at the cover. My co-author is Larry Deibert. He is my friend and I have known him for about eight years. *(I actually had the pleasure of knowing Riley for about 12 and a half years.-Larry)*

I wanted to write this book myself without any help, but it's a little too tough for a dog to sit at a computer typing for the length of time it takes to write a book. I asked Larry if he'd do all the writing and I would tell him what to write.

So, okay, maybe I told a little white lie there, since dogs can't really talk, but I think I communicate pretty much everything that's going to be written on these pages, so just bear with us and I hope we'll be able to entertain you.

I was born in December of 2000, and my home was in a crate at a pet shop called Pets Plus in Quakertown, Pennsylvania. One day, a nice young man, Sean, and his mother, Peggy, came and took me home. I was very happy.

Sean trained me very well to be a good puppy, and I tried hard, although there were more than a few things I did wrong. Hey, I had a lot to learn about living in the world of people. It was going to be better than being locked in a pet store all night, and getting fondled by people all day long. Sometimes the barking, meowing, bird sounds, and whatever was so unpleasant it made my sleeping difficult.

So let's begin when I met him.

2

I used to listen in on Peggy's telephone conversations, and more and more I kept hearing about this guy named Larry. I knew Peggy was a little lonely because she needed someone her age to have fun with and the way everything sounded, this guy just might be who she would need for a companion. At that time, I didn't know much about relationships between men and women, just between a mom and her son.

Anyway-I say that a lot and I'm sorry about that-but, anyway, one night Peggy went out with this guy, Larry, and I think she really liked him because after she came home, she called him and they talked on the phone for pretty long. I tried to sleep, but she sounded so happy, her joy kept me awake for a long time. Finally she hung up and then she petted me. "Riley, someday soon, you're going to meet a very nice man and I hope you like him.

It took me a while to fall asleep because so many things were going through my head about this guy, Larry, and true to her word, one night he was invited over to watch TV with us and I was so excited to meet him.

3

The night finally came and I sat at the balcony door, watching and waiting for him to show up.

Each time I saw a car come down Mansfield Street, which runs in front of our second floor condo, I'd stand up and bark, alerting Peggy, but when the car didn't stop, I had to try to get comfortable again and wait.

I was almost asleep at the window, when I heard an engine and I quickly stood up and looked out. It was a car I had never seen before, a minivan, and when it pulled into a parking space across the street, I started barking when I saw a man get out and walk toward my door. When he was no longer in sight, meaning he was approaching the door, I stood at the landing, looking down. I guess Peggy must have left the door unlocked because I heard it open and then I heard footsteps on the carpeted stairs. I could see his profile and when he got to the landing and turned to face us, I started wagging my tail and barking happily.

He came upstairs and started petting me and talking to me, something he would do thousands of times, and I never tired of him doing this.

Peggy and Larry sat beside each other on the sofa and I curled up beside Larry and took a nap.

A slight movement awakened me and although I didn't know what was going to happen, I saw Larry's face turn toward Peggy. Not wanting to miss anything, I jumped up on the back of the sofa and got between them. Next thing I knew I was getting a snookie, which is a kiss, by both of them on each side of my face. They must really like me a lot I thought.

Peggy and Larry both laughed like crazy and then they played with me, passing me back and forth between them, rubbing my back and my belly, with many, many more snookies before we all settled down to watch a movie.

Time passed so quickly and Larry had to leave because he was a mailman and had to get up early to go to work the next morning.

He kissed Peggy on the lips and then bent down and kissed me on the top of the head. "Riley, I'll see you soon. Okay?"

I danced a little and then he left.

I watched him get in his car and leave.

Little did I know that someday Larry would become my caretaker and do so many things for me until I would have to leave them. Fortunately that wouldn't be for over 12 more years.

4

Whenever he would come over to see Peggy, he and I would bond. He'd take me out for a walk, especially if he and Peggy were just going to hang out at the house and watch TV.

We'd go down in the field and he'd unleash me. I'd take off running, sniffing the ground, chasing moths, and of course, doing my business. Usually that didn't take too long because I was just so excited to both see him and be outside off the leash.

During the day, when nobody was home, I had to stay in the crate in the kitchen and that imprisonment was really beginning to upset me. So, what does a dog do when he is upset? You got it, he cries and whines. That really didn't help me out too much, since nobody was there to hear me. Eventually, I decided that sleeping would be a much better activity, so that's what I did.

Eventually I was released from daytime captivity and had a free run of the house. I always was careful not to have any accidents while Peggy and Sean were at work, and by the fall, Larry was staying at the house more often and Sean decided it was time to get his own place.

We moved into a house on a golf course, so I was able to see people playing that game sometime. I sure wished I could have run around on the golf course because it was so big.

I was happy that we were moving, but I was really sad too, knowing that I wouldn't see Peggy and Larry as often.

They came up with the idea of me spending two weeks with Sean and then two weeks at Society Hill with Larry, Peggy, and all my human and dog friends.

Of course, I was very happy with that arrangement. I loved Sean a lot, because he trained me from the time he brought me home, teaching me all the cool things a dog should know to please other peops. But when it was time to stay with Larry and Peggy, I was really excited.

I can't remember what year it was, nor how old I was, but Sean moved to another place to live, near a town called Bensalem. It was well over and hour's drive from Hellertown, and perhaps a little less from where Sean and I had lived near Trexlertown.

Peggy and Larry didn't get me as often now, and when they wanted me, they often had to drive all that way to get me, and then Sean would usually come up after a couple of weeks, sometimes more, to take me back home.

5

About six years ago, Sean bought a house, and that made it easier for me to spend time with both human couples. His house was only about forty-five minutes from Hellertown, so Larry would meet Sean at a point about halfway between the towns and I'd hop from his car into Larry's.

Before I'd get in the backseat, I would jump and bark, so happy to see him, knowing that for two weeks, at least, I would get a nice walk in the morning before he had to go to work. At that time Larry was working five hours a day, five days a week, but soon he was going to start a new shift, working only Monday, Tuesday and Wednesday, and then he had four days off; four days where he spent a lot of quality time with me and I was really happy.

6

Sometime in 2012, I think, I was really starting to have trouble with my back and my legs. Sean had hardwood floors in the kitchen, living room, dining room, and the entrance way.

One day he came home from work and I was splayed out under the dining room table, unable to grip the wood floors to stand up.

Sean called Peggy and asked if she and Larry would consider being my caretaker for the rest of my life and Larry didn't hesitate one bit, even though they didn't want a full time dog.

The love that man showed me over the remainder of the time I had on earth, was more than any dog could ever hope for.

Anyway, I'm not going to get too maudlin about my final years, because he made me as comfortable as possible. I have been a very lucky dog, having them love me so much.

I was only a couple of years old when this was taken. The day was extremely sunny, offering Larry and I a great walk outside.

Moths, Fireflies and a Bat

1

The first time Peggy and Larry took me to the Murray Goodman Campus of Lehigh University, I jumped from the back seat and Larry had to restrain me because I just wanted to run and jump and have the kind of fun a dog can have off the leash. We all knew it wasn't legal to let me run free, but so many people did it with their dogs, that the College cops usually looked the other way.

Anyway-darn, there I go again-we crossed the road and I went under the little rail fence bordering the huge field we would play in. Larry and Peggy stepped over the fence and then he kneeled down and took off my leash. "Riley, you be a good boy," he said.

Off I ran and I had only gone about fifty feet when a humongous amount of pretty, tasty, little moths took flight. I bet there were hundreds. Maybe even thousands, of them. I chased them, jumping as high as I could, sometimes landing so off balance that I would tumble and roll around.

I could hear Larry and Peggy laughing as they tried to catch up with me, but I couldn't even pay attention to them because the moths were always beckoning me to chase them by flitting closer and closer to the grass and to me. I don't even remember if I caught any but I had probably about fifteen minutes of mind-blowing, doggy fun.

Over all the years that Larry took me for walks where he could leave me off the leash, I chased many moths and I also tried to chase birds and squirrels. Larry would say, "Riley, you can't chase birds because they're too fast and they fly too high." He'd also say, "Ri, you can't chase squirrels because they're too fast and they climb trees." I'd look at him as though he was crazy, but I always realized he was right. Just some things a dog can't do.

2

Yesterday, Larry, took me out for a walk where I didn't have to be restrained by a leash. I hate leashes, don't you? Anyway, we were having a really good time. He was watching me eat grass and run around and alongside him, because he was afraid I was getting old. You see, the night before yesterday, I tried to hurry up and down the stairs because we live on a second floor condo and I kinda fell down. Well, I am going on ten and my legs sometimes don't work as well as they used to when I was just a pup. I think Larry took me out on this walk not only to see how well my legs would respond, but also to run a little bit himself. If you see his wife, Peggy, don't tell her that he was running or we'll both probably be in trouble.

Okay, where was I? Oh yes, I remember now. We went over to a really cool walking path near the college football field. There are so many dogs that are walked and run there that the smells left behind on the ground, bushes, and trees are too much to pass up, so sometimes it takes us quite a while to get moving.

Nearly midway into our run/walk, I spotted this huge white moth and I lit out after it, jumping as high as I could to catch it. I jump pretty high for an old dog, but the moths generally fly just a little out of my reach. I think they do this, not only because they can, but because they like to add a little excitement to their lives, which aren't very long. While Larry was writing this for me he looked it up and found that a Luna moth, whatever that is, lives only about a week, while other species live a couple or three weeks. I really didn't care too much when he told me (he talks to me all the time) all I really care about is the thrill of the chase. If I get to swallow one, that is a bonus.

I could see Larry watching me with a smile on his face. He realized that I was okay and wasn't going to keel over anytime soon. I have to find a way to let him know he shouldn't watch sad movies about dogs and worry about me all the time. Unfortunately, I didn't catch this one particular moth, so I went back to sniffing all the good stuff on the grass, bushes and trees again. During the course of our walk, I spotted and chased eight moths and you better believe I was really pooped when we finished and I climbed back in the car for the ride home. When Larry went golfing later in the afternoon, I took a really long nap until Peggy came home from work.

3

Several years ago, I had one of the best treats a moth chasing dog could possibly receive. It was early evening when Peggy and Larry took me to another area in the same complex where we walk now.

Anyway, they guided me to a huge field and when they took my leash off, I began to run around, sniffing as I usually do, when hundreds of moths became airborne in a very short time. I must have chased them for ten minutes or more. My peops watched in total amusement and amazement I might add. I could really jump in those days because I think I was only about three or four at the time. Man, I was soooo fast back then.

I remember a time when I was living with Sean, in a house near a golf course. It was a cool place to live because when I was outside in a fenced in yard, I could watch the peops play golf and listen to them yell about their bad shots. That was fun. Oh, you will see the word peops a lot-my word for people.

There was a small bush in the yard and I would sometimes hide behind it and wait for a moth to come fluttering nearby. As soon as one would come close, I would pounce out from behind that old bush and chase the little critter until it flew away or ended up in my belly. Yum! I gotta admit that I haven't swallowed more than a handful or so in my lifetime, but I keep trying.

4

Okay, I guess that's enough about moths for the time being. I may pick up on it later when I talk about the outdoor gatherings we have with all the dog peops. Well, I guess I'll talk a little about that now, but only as far as chasing flying things go.

In our community there is a little field where we used to run free most of the time, until a couple of unfortunate incidents and the peops had to put us back on the leashes. I'll have a really good story about that a little later on, gang.

So one night we're all out there hanging out. The peops are sitting around the picnic table or in folding chairs having a few drinks and some snacks. That's another subject to cover later because I need to tell you all that we dogs are really pigs sometimes and never stop eating human food. It's really good.

I was running around as the sun began to set and I saw a little light hovering just above the blades of grass. The light went out and I got into a defensive stance to protect all my friends, both human and dog, from this never before seen sight. At least it was never before seen by me. As I watched, the light blinked on again and I started barking, moving about from side to side and front to back, waiting for the light to go on again. Larry must have heard me bark and he walked toward me. I looked at him, wishing I could talk and tell him to get away until I figured out what the strange light was.

We both saw it again less than a minute later, but now there were several of them and I was quite startled. Darn near gave me a heart attack, just like the times I saw my first rabbit and cat. Larry laughed as I took off snapping at the lights.

"Hey guys," he yelled out to the other peops, "check out Riley chasing fireflies."

I was so embarrassed knowing that the peops knew what these lights were and I didn't. Now knowing that they didn't pose a threat to our survival, I just continued having fun chasing them, trying to figure out where they'd be when they glowed again. It was a successful hunt that night; I think I caught and swallowed at least fifteen of the little bugs. They were tasty, but not very satisfying.

Later on, I began chasing another threat, and all the peops were wondering what I was after. None of the other dogs paid any attention to the black thing in the sky, but I wasn't going to let that flying creature do any harm to my loved ones. I must have chased it and jumped up to snag it out of the air for a really long time because I was getting pretty tired, and hungry. As I was ready to give up the ghost on this chase one of the peops yelled out, "Riley's chasing a bat." I had no idea what a bat was: still don't, but I would imagine if I caught one, it'd be pretty tasty.

By now it was completely dark and there was nothing flying about anymore, so I joined my furry and non-furry friends at the picnic table. After getting a huge drink of water and eating a couple of crackers and some cheese, I was ready for a nap until the party broke up and we went home to my really favorite place-Larry and Peggy's bed.

Since I just mentioned that, I guess I'll tell you about it.

I have always been a bed dog, so I'd jump up and circle around on top of the cover, settling in while Peggy and Larry watched TV.

Sometimes I would stand up and stare at Larry until he lifted the quilt and the sheet so I could get under and snuggle head first against his leg. If I stretched out, Peggy would sometimes get mad because I'd almost push her out of bed with my back feet. I guess there were times that they both got mad at the sleeping arrangement, but, hey, it was always all about me.

After a certain amount of time, I would get hot, and quite honestly, the air could get a little stuffy under there. I would literally jump up, nearly exploding out from under the covers and go to the bottom of the bed, under the fan, where it was nice and cool.

Life was really good.

.

Riley laying on the bed, probably watching Peggy iron. He slept with us almost every night until he got really old and was unable to jump up. I would sometimes lift him up and set him down, but he would stand up and carefully jump down. I think he became afraid that he might fall off the bed. He decided to spend most of his sleeping time in the living room, on the floor.

Riley loved his Frosty Paws. He would get one almost every night around 8:30. Often times he did a puppy dance in front of me, letting me know it was time for his treat. His other favorite ice cream type of treat was a cup of soft vanilla yogurt from Rita's. Many times they stuck a doggie bone in the top, making it a doggie sundae.

Frosty Paws, Frozen Yogurt, and Other Treats

Two of my favorite treats in the world are Frosty Paws and Frozen Yogurt custard from Rita's

Usually, every night around eight thirty, Larry will get up from his chair, or the sofa, alerting me that it is time for my treat. I'll look at him and he says, "Riley, are you ready for a Frosty Paw?" I would jump up when I was young, but in the past few months, because of my arthritis, it took my some time to get up. He heads out to the kitchen and opens the freezer door. I know what's going to come out of there. Yummy! He grabs a Frosty Paw, pulls off the top and pretends that he is going to eat it. When I was younger, I used to jump up and down several times, trying to take the little white cardboard cup from his hand, then I would bark a couple of times and wag my tail. He'd tell me to sit and then he would set the cup on the floor. I'd pick it up with my teeth and carry it off to the living room where I could lick the frozen protein puppy ice cream to my heart's content. Well, actually I can only lick until it is gone and you'd think I'd be satisfied, but I never seem to be. I always want more. Over the past few weeks before I went to sleep, there were times I couldn't even finish it because I didn't have enough energy left.

Then there are the really nice occasions when we take a walk through town, generally on a side street where lots of dogs have walked leaving their marks behind for me to sniff. Larry would guide me right to the window of Rita's and I would go nuts jumping up and down and barking because I know what I'm going to get.

Larry usually shortens my extender leash and ties me to a post and then he sits down on the concrete patio outside the place while Peggy waits in line to get our treats. They almost always get cones of the soft goodie but my vanilla treat is always in a small container.

Sometimes I have to wait really long before she brings it over and Larry places it between his sneakers, shoes or sandals depending on how warm it is. I can hardly contain myself as he sets it down on the pavement before my tongue is doing a dance on the sweet treat. I must confess that I become really piggish as I gobble it down, usually in less than a couple of minutes. Sometimes the girls working there would put a little crunchy doggie bone treat in the yogurt and it would stand up. I'd just eat around it and save it for last

When I lifted my head, Peggy and Larry sometimes laughed because there is vanilla all over my nose and the fur around my mouth. I just start licking and before you know it, all the leftover goodness winds up in my belly.

I sit and watch them finish their cones and I also watch all the people coming and going, hoping that they might give me some too.

Next door to the frozen yogurt stand is a pizza place and I gotta admit that I love pizza as well.

When Peggy and Larry get hungry for pizza, he usually takes the car to drive there to pick up a pie. Most times he will take me along and I stand in the back seat until we get there. He locks me in the car and says, "Riley, I'll be right back. You be a good boy, okay!"

Well what else can I do but be a good boy. There's nothing in the car for me to eat. I have nothing to play with either. All I usually do is just hang out and rest my chin on the top of the back seat looking around to see if anyone comes near the car. Sometimes people come up to the window and say, "Nice dog." I usually smile and wag my tail. Sometimes I wish I was left outside to greet people and maybe have them give me a little snack, but I don't want anyone to take me.

When Larry would get back into the car, the smell of pizza drove me crazy and I whined and barked, wanting some now, but I knew I always had to wait until we got home. Larry would park the car, let me out first, because when we went for pizza, I was usually off the leash. He'd get the pizza and I'd jump and howl, just wanting it so bad because it smelled so good.

Once in the house, after I literally tore up the stairs and ran around in circles, he'd put the pizza on the kitchen counter, take a couple of slices and put them on a plate. I'd follow him back into the living room and, like a sentry, I'd stand in front of him, watching him eat, hoping some would drop. As soon as Peggy had her slices, I'd go to her and she was usually the first one who'd give me a small piece of the crust. She'd toss it and sometimes I'd catch it in mid-air, nearly having it swallowed before my paws touched the carpet again.

Then I'd go back to Larry, and because he ate faster, which was not a good thing, and I wish he'd take more time to enjoy his food-whoa! I can't believe I said that because the time food rests on my tongue and teeth is so minimal. Anyway, I wait and then he tears up little pieces of crust and tosses them near me or over my head, making me work for my meal. I don't care, though, because they always give me more until they finish eating.

TV time is always good because sometimes there is popcorn, or potato chips, or pretzels. I also like tortilla chips.

I may have said this before, but I really love McDonald's French fries. Peggy and Larry always have to get a large order for them and me to share.

Riley would often times empty his bucket of toys and root around until he found what he wanted to play with. You can see the empty bucket off to the right near the top of the picture.

Sometimes his favorite toy was an empty plastic water bottle, which he would carry around in his mouth, toss it in the air, chase it and do that over and over again. Often times, I tried to steal it from him. He would run and hide, watching me from the corner of his eye. I would do it again and again. We had great fun with this.

A Bucket Full Of Toys

Whether it is a bucket, a basket, or a box, the container of choice holds a dog's toys. Old ones and new ones rest happily in my bucket until I am able to knock it over by latching on to the top with my paw or push it over with my nose. My toys spill out on the floor and I can choose any one I wish to play with.

There are times when none of the toys float my boat and then I'll whine a little bit to get some attention, hoping that Larry or Peggy will take me outside so I can sniff all the good scents on the ground and maybe see some of my friends. I hate to be bored, but most of a dog's life is just lying around the house waiting for the next bowl of food, the next playtime, or the next walk outside.

However, I am drifting away from the subject of this chapter, which is toys. Like I said, I have a lot of toys but many of them have no meaning to me anymore and I just brush by them, hoping to find one that will entertain me for a while. For some unknown reason, Larry and Peggy put the kerchiefs I am given after a bath at a really cool dog grooming place in the bucket, but they rarely put them around my neck again

I have an assortment of rubber balls of different shapes and sizes, rawhide and nylon chew bones of different shapes and sizes, rope, a stuffed monkey from which I already tore out the stuffing and chewed off one leg, both arms and an ear, and a stuffed elephant which is in pretty much the same condition as the monkey.

Out of the corner of my eye, I spied an old miniature rubber football that I stole from a dog I knew. This is always fun to chew on especially since there is no air in the toy.

I really enjoy lying on the living room floor chewing on a thin rawhide stick. I use it to clean my teeth by moving it from one side of the mouth to the other. Sometimes Larry teases me, saying, "Ri, I'm gonna get that bone." Then we have a little fun as he chases me and I hide under the dining room table or simply outmaneuver him. It's easy for a little dog like me to keep my distance, even though I know he won't take my bone and just wants to play with me a little.

One time, however, a few years ago I had the knotted end of a large rawhide bone in my mouth and it got stuck. I was worried that I wouldn't be able to get it out, so Larry held my jaws open with one hand and reached in to pull out the piece that was stuck. When he got it out, I involuntarily closed my mouth and nearly bit him. I would have been really sad if that had happened.

My truly favorite toy of all time, got broken some time ago and that was really upsetting. It was this big plastic ball that made noises when it rolled. It's been gone for so long that I don't remember what the noises were, but I think it was Sean's voice telling me something. Anyway, Larry or Peggy would fill it with dry dog food and as it rolled or I pushed it with my nose or paws, wonderful brown nuggets would spill out and I would eat and eat, and roll the ball until all the food was gone and I had to move on to something else.

After Peggy or Larry made little turkey or chicken pot pies in the oven, they would scrape the food onto a plate. The aluminum containers they came in were perfect for me to try to get every bit of food out of them. Of course, these containers became toys since I would push them and turn them upside down and then back again, trying to get every bit of crust, meat, or gravy that remained in the grooves of the containers. Usually there were four of them to keep me busy, and this also gave Peggy and Larry time to eat.

After I got out everything I could from the containers, or they wound up out of my reach, so to speak, I'd head back into the living room and there on the floor would be the plates with a little leftover food on them. I used to lick them so clean that Larry would tell Peggy he was going to just put them away without washing them. "Look, Peggy. Ri cleaned these so well, I don't need to put them in the dishwasher."

She would shake her finger at him and then they both laughed. I was so happy I could entertain them.

There were several times that one of my peops would bring home large balloons that were filled with helium. There was always a long ribbon attached to them and I'd try my darndest to grab the ribbon with my paw to bring the balloon down to earth, where I could bat it with my paws and growl and bark at it if it began to float upward toward the ceiling again. That was great fun for a dog and Larry liked to tease me by moving the balloon real close to me as I laid in attack mode, ready to spring on the balloon, much like I would leap toward a moth just hovering over the grass.

I also liked to play with plastic milk containers because it would be fun to chew into the plastic and eventually tear it apart. I think I liked to do this because there was still a coating of milk on the inside and, well, anyway, you already know my feelings about food and drink.

A Visit To The Vet

Several years ago, I gave Larry and Peggy a little scare over the Memorial Day holiday.

Larry has a part-time job and he only works on Monday, Tuesday and Wednesday. His off time includes a lot of time spent with me and I hardly nap during that time frame. Well, I guess with a shortage of sleep and more outside time, I wore myself a little thin and I couldn't sit down.

I heard Larry call the vet and make an appointment to see her after he returned home from work the day after Memorial Day. After he left for work that morning, I guess I was so tired; I laid on the bed and fell asleep. I heard Peggy call my name but I didn't respond to her so she became worried about me.

Finally she came over and sat beside me and I lifted my head. She was so happy because I think she thought I had died. I must have really been sleeping soundly. She gave me hugs and kisses, but all I wanted was sleep.

When she left to go to work, I was lying on the living room floor in a kind of la la land. Have any of you ever stared into space like you were in a trance? Well, I did, and I didn't even get up to give her any snookies before she left.

I must have slept all morning because the next thing I remember was I heard a neighbor calling me from the street below our window. She must have awakened me because I responded by getting up and going to the balcony door and I barked at her. I was wagging my tail too, but I guess she didn't see that. I thought she was going to come in and play with me or give me a treat to eat. When she walked away, I laid down again and fell asleep for a couple of hours until Larry finally came home from work.

We were so happy to see each other, but I was more excited to go outside to do my business after being in the house alone for over eight hours. We took a walk and Larry told me we were going to see the vet.

Oh, I forgot to tell you why he made an appointment. Well, I was unable to sit down for a day or so because my back hurt. All

Larry's peops gave him different opinions of what could have happened to me and what he should do to help relieve me of the pain I was in, but he didn't listen to any of their advice, preferring to leave the diagnosis up to a professional.

We got in the car and took the short ride to the animal hospital and when he walked me to the door I started to get a little upset. I really don't like going into that place because I know I'm going to get poked and prodded in places I don't care to get poked and prodded, but it's the only way a peop can find out what's wrong with the animal patient. If only we could talk, life would be so much easier.

Anyway, Larry took me from the car and we walked to the front door of the animal hospital. As soon as I saw where we were going, I turned around and started to pull Larry back toward the car with me. I was having no part of that place, because of the poking and prodding. After a moment of thought, however, I realized that I wouldn't be able to get fixed without going in. I knew what was wrong with me, but Larry and Peggy didn't have a clue because they sometimes don't understand what I'm trying to say.

Once inside, I settled down a little. Larry and a nurse helped get me onto the scale. I was pretty happy because I had lost almost four pounds since my last visit in the winter. Those Saturday and Sunday morning walks were finally beginning to pay off as a health issue. Plus, the weekends always give me more opportunities to chase more moths.

Once the weigh-in was complete, we went into an examination room. Larry sat down in a chair and I sat on the floor. He looked at me and looked at the nurse, and then back at me again.

"Riley, I thought you couldn't sit?" he inquired, puzzled.

The nurse had seen that I didn't sit correctly, and she knew something was wrong. Anyway, she asked him a lot of questions as I eyed the peanut butter jar or the counter. I knew I'd never be able to get up on that counter, but I could smell that the jar had been recently opened. I stretched my neck and also saw there was an open bag of dog treats as well and saliva began doing its job. I was getting awfully hungry.

The nurse left the room and all Larry and I could do was wait until the vet would come in to check me out. I lay down on the floor, wondering if Larry would sneak a finger full of peanut butter for me, or perhaps one or two of the wonderful smelling treats. If peops would know how those scents drive us wild, they would keep all foods tightly sealed.

A few minutes later, the vet and the nurse stepped in the examination room and they, along with Larry, helped me get on the stainless steel examination table. That was pretty cool because they were able to lower the table toward the floor and then the table started rising to a height where the vet was able to check me out without bending over.

I was pretty excited so my heart rate was pretty high. My temperature was elevated as well, but the vet said it could be from nervousness. That sure was right, because I knew what was going to happen next, since the nurse put a muzzle on me. I hate those things.

She put her finger where fingers shouldn't be put and, well, I'll spare you all the details, but it was not a pleasant experience.

"Riley's blocked up and we're going to take him to the treatment room to clean him out." The vet told Larry.

A few minutes later I was reunited with Larry and I felt a million percent better. They gave Larry a few meds for me to take and we went back home to have fun again.

I sure don't want to have to go through that again.

Riley always looked so good after his bath and haircut. No matter where I took him, the staff always gave him the exact cut that I wanted

Getting Groomed

1

The time had come for a professional bath and my summer haircut. I do like the aftermath of the grooming experience, but I'm not super fond of the cutting and the bathing by strangers.

Larry dropped me off at the grooming place and then left. I found out later that he had breakfast with his son and then ran a couple of errands before he came to pick me up. I was in that place for over three hours with a few other dogs and he arrived before they had finished my haircut.

I went a little nuts when I saw him because I was sooo ready to go and get something to eat and drink. I was really hungry and thirsty.

Anyway, few minutes later, I was ushered out to the waiting room, wearing a bandanna around my neck, signifying that I had a haircut. I was so happy to be finished that I jumped up on Larry and gave him a ton of snookies. He was happy to see me too and scratched me behind my ears for a little bit while the lady wrote up the bill. Oh, I forgot, they cut my nails, too, and that was good because they were getting a little too long.

We went home in the car and then took a walk around the community. Everyone who saw me commented on how good I looked and how nice I smelled. A summer cut is really good because when I go swimming in the creek, it is much easier for Larry to towel me dry. I really like getting dried off with a towel because it feels good, especially on my belly.

2

Larry has given me showers at home and let me tell you, that is not an easy process.

He has to get in the shower with me and then he has to move out of the way of the spray of water so I can get good and wet before he squirts on some doggie shampoo and tries to work it in with his hands. I know he is trying, but sometimes he misses some spots and when the shower is finished, I am not completely clean.

Larry will lift my front legs and rest my paws on him so that he can really rub down my back and tail and get a lot of my undercarriage. That's what he calls my belly.

Once I am all lathered up, then he has to move around again, so that the water can hit me for my rinsing.

After that is all done, Larry shuts off the water and reaches outside the shower to grab a towel to begin drying me off. When he lets me out of the shower, I begin to shake off some of the water and it sprays all over the bathroom floor. He finishes toweling me off and then he has to clean up the mess I left behind.

3

In summertime it is so much easier because he will take me down to a friend's house and shampoos me and hoses me off outside. After he washes me with some doggie soap and water, I love getting rinsed off. The clear, cool water feels so good on my fur. Then we head home for the really fun part of a bath. Larry gets a couple of towels and dries me. When he thinks he's finished, I always stare at him for a minute or two and when he picks up the towels again, I dance in a couple of circles and bark until he towels me off some more. It feels so good.

Early Morning Walks

When Larry went on the Weight Watchers program, he decided to take one hour walks before work. This was when he was still working the five hour day, five days a week shift. He started work around 9 AM so we would take our walks around 6, or just as the sun was coming up. This was one of my favorite things to do and I loved the early morning because the air was so fresh and clean.

He'd say, "Ri wanna go for a walk?" I start going nuts, barking and turning in circles, but he makes me wait until he has a cup of coffee first. At least he programs the coffee maker so that I don't have to wait until it perks. After a cup, he grabs his cassette player and my leash and we head out the door.

Larry varies the route we take so that he doesn't get bored walking the same way every day. I don't understand this at all, because pretty much everything looks the same when your head is only about a foot off the ground, but I really don't care, as long as I am able to go out with him and sniff my way around a three-and-a half to four mile walk.

Sometimes we see deer running around. One day several deer watched us go by. I think the little one, they call them fawns, thought I was a deer too because he started edging closer until he was only about fifteen feet away. We kept watching him and as we passed by, Larry kept looking over his shoulder and the deer just stood there watching us. When we turned around to head home, we passed by them again. The fawn came toward us and when we were about twenty yards past, the fawn that was watching us went back to the bigger older deer. Larry stopped and turned around to watch them nuzzle each other and hop around the field. That was great fun for both of us.

We always have to be careful because, even at that early hour, there are cars moving up and down the road, probably people on their way to work, so Larry always makes sure that we are well out of their way as they pass by.

Most of the times we walked, I would pull Larry because it seemed as though he was going to slow. The last few times I went for a long walk with him, maybe a year and a half ago, I was beginning to feel my age and generally I would lag behind.

I know there is a country music song where the singer says he's not as good as he once was, but he's as good once as he ever was. Sometimes I still felt like that at the age of 12 or 13, but the times were few and far between.

Riley enjoyed Christmas very much. Not only did he get lots of table treats, but he had his own stocking and sometimes it was filled with treats and toys. He would pick it up and shake it, trying to get all the goodies out. If he smelled something really good, he would jump high in the air, again, and again, until one of us tore the wrapper off and gave it to him.

Riley and I on Christmas, 2013.

Holidays and Get-Togethers

1

I've always liked holidays. Often when Sean, Peg and Larry got together with Nana and Vinnie, we were one happy family.

During the summer there would be picnics with lots of food and all the dogs would be able to sample some of the people food that was being served. I grew particularly fond of hot dogs, hamburgers, potato chips, pretzels; who am I kidding, I liked everything that the peops would eat, although I was never given any chocolate, because chocolate can be deadly to a dog. Other than that, everything would be yummy. Until the day that the police visited one of our picnics, we dogs were always allowed to run free and play with one another. I never played much but I did like to dig holes and eat dirt.

Anyway, on this particular day, both dogs and peops were having a great time. The peops were drinking beer and wine, but not to excess as far as I could tell. Apparently, someone drove by and saw us running free and had a cow (pardon the animal joke; I still can't figure out what that means when peops say it, but that's what they say sometimes.) Soon after, a policeman arrived, but just before he was in sight, all of we dogs went back to the table and laid down at the feet of our people. The leashes were nearby and as soon as the officer was spotted, we were all hooked up before he came to the picnic table.

Larry said, "Good evening Officer, how are you?"

He nodded and said, "I was called away from dinner by a report that a bunch of drunken people were letting their dogs run loose, but none of you appear intoxicated and the dogs are hooked up, so I don't see a problem. I will have a talk with the person who called in the nuisance report." He scowled. "Frankly I am quite annoyed because I was on my break celebrating my wedding anniversary with my wife, having a nice dinner."

"Sorry you were sent out here, Officer", one person said, "And Happy Anniversary." Everyone then wished him and his wife a Happy Anniversary.

"Thanks. I'm heading back now to finish my dinner. You all have a great night." He hopped in his car and left.

Peops will never know it, but we knew the police were going to come before they did, and we knew what we had to do so no one got into trouble.

2

My favorite holidays are Thanksgiving and Christmas. On Thanksgiving there is always a great feast and then usually the men will watch football and the women will sit around and talk. I like watching football, but Sean and Larry are always 'trash talking'. They seem to have a great deal of fun doing this, and I usually lie between them and get a heavy dose of petting and ear scratching at this time.

During the days and weeks after Thanksgiving, Peg and Larry are always busy with Christmas shopping (Sometimes I get to go along and sniff out other peops and animals. Occasionally I will find a treat laying on the pavement and that makes the shopping trips extra special.) Then they go through the chore of bringing all the tubs down from the attic that contains their Christmas decorations and lights and they begin to turn our house into a Christmas wonderland. At one point, Larry counted twenty-three tubs, bags and boxes filled with decorations. They have Clothique Santas, Pipkas-which are hand painted figurines-garland, lights, pictures, and lots of other stuff. Peggy has been saying for years that she was not going to put out all her decorations, but she usually does. For some reason, this year everything looked extra special when I came home again, after my customary two weeks with Sean.

3

Sean arrived in the late afternoon on Christmas Eve, and he was really happy to see me. He also liked the little Santa hat and red and white bell collar that I was wearing. I was surprised because Sean generally doesn't like to see me wearing stuff other than my fur. One year Larry put a Dallas Cowboys t-shirt around my back and belly and I thought he was going to freak out. "Get that off my dog," he yelled. You see, Sean is a Green Bay Packers fan, so he was not amused.

I watched while they opened presents and played the white elephant Christmas game. That game is fun because each person tries to come up with a gift that is completely ludicrous or funny. Each person draws a number, and then based on the numbers the person selects and opens the gift. The next person has an opportunity to steal that gift or open a new one. After all the gifts are opened, numbers are drawn again and the each person in succession has an opportunity to change or keep gifts. Usually while they are doing this, I get a little snack. This year I had several tasty treats in my stocking and that is the most fun part of opening gifts.

Larry was shocked when he saw one of the white elephant gifts was his favorite, well, his only, Dallas Cowboys sweatshirt. Fortunately, he was able to get it back. Vinnie was shocked one time because when someone opened the gift they chose, it was Vinnie's wooden cereal bowl. We all laughed and he shook his finger at Nana for sneaking it out of the house. He got it back, though.

After gifts are opened, we sit down for dinner. I usually sit at Vinnie's feet because he feeds me all the time. He tries to be discreet, but Sean usually catches him in the act.

Later on, after church there were more treats before we went to sleep.

Larry always cooks Christmas breakfast, so I was able to munch on some eggs, toast and bacon. I really love bacon; I love it so much, I jumped high off the floor, hoping that my acrobatics would reward me with more. Yum.

Bad Dog/Good Dog

1

I really loved taking walks around the Murray-Goodman campus of Lehigh University when there were sporting events going on.

During lacrosse season, teams come in from all over the country, I think, and there are many tents and things set up where the peops hang out until their teams are playing. Sometimes they bring their dogs with them and, although we all keep our distance, they are pretty much thinking the same thing-so much food and so many good smells of those foods.

I usually pull on the leash, trying to get closer to the places the people are sitting, hoping one or more of them would toss me a sliver of something good. It rarely happens, but some people have come over to pet me while we were walking through, mainly because no matter how old I get, I am so darn cute. They'll stop and pet me and if they have a dog, they'll give me a doggie treat. Larry calls me the biggest beggar boy on the planet, and he ain't wrong.

During football season, people are tailgating, cooking all kinds of good things on their grills and the scent of all that food sometimes makes me swoon, but we don't visit any of these places, even though I think Larry gets hungry too, sometimes.

One day, about two weeks after a football game, we were walking along. Larry was listening to his music and I was dawdling behind him a little bit, sniffing the ground. When I saw it, I knew I had to have it, so I stopped, alerting Larry that something was amiss.

He turned around just in time to see something go into my mouth but he didn't know what it was. He pulled me closer and tried to make me spit out what I had, but I was adamant. I was going to eat this snack and I didn't care how long it would take, or so I thought.

Larry kept pulling me, not allowing any slack in the leash so I could sit down and enjoy the treat firmly held inside my mouth. It was driving me crazy and I thought I'd never get a chance to chew and then swallow the wonderful goodness hidden from his view.

We walked all the rest of the way home, him pulling me, not allowing me the opportunity to eat and I was not a happy camper.

Once we neared Society Hill, I saw him take his cell phone from his pocket and he called a neighbor.

"Riley has something in his mouth and I don't want him to eat it because I don't know what it is. Could you bring a couple of treats out and maybe when you show them to him, he'll spit the thing out." I heard him say that, and I knew I would have a tough decision to make.

We got to her house and she showed me the wonderful treats that I could have if I would just spit out what I had in my mouth. By now, I really couldn't smell what was in my mouth anymore and the treats that looked and smelled like bacon were making my mouth water.

I acquiesced and spit out the item, jumping up for the bacon like treats.

What I spat out made Larry and his friend almost gag. It was about half of a hot dog in a roll that had already turned green, but to me, when I found it, the hot dog seemed like the best thing a dog could ever have.

I think Larry threatened that I would lose my nose if I ever did that again. He has told me that before, but I don't think he would ever cut my nose off, but I better be careful I guess.

2

One time, I watched Larry make a ham and cheese sandwich in the kitchen. I stood there, looking all the way up at him until he'd toss me a little piece of ham and some cheese to satisfy my beggar boy mode, which it seems I'm always in.

He brought his sandwich and a handful of potato chips into the living room and set the plate down on the coffee table. I think he was watching a baseball or a football game, or perhaps it was a golf tournament.

Larry sat down and took a sip of beer. Once he gave me a taste of beer, but I didn't like it so I never begged for that. He picked up the sandwich and I watched him open his mouth and take a small bite, then he put the sandwich down on the plate. I never took my eye of that sandwich.

As he chewed, the doorbell rang. Since he was sitting on the sofa and not in his favorite chair by the window, he couldn't tell if anyone had pulled up in a car, or if it might be a neighbor taking a walk and then stopping by to chat with my friend.

He stood up and then turned back to me. "Ri, don't you dare touch that sandwich." He walked down the stairs and opened the door, looking out. Nobody was there, so he opened the door and stepped outside, still seeing nobody.

He came back upstairs and saw me sitting by the window, looking out.

When he looked at the coffee table, the chips were still there, but the sandwich had somehow found its way into my belly. I couldn't help it.

Larry didn't talk to me the rest of the day and after Peggy came home from her shopping trip he told her what I had done. She thought it was pretty funny and told him to start talking to me again. He did, but he wasn't too happy about the outcome with his sandwich and with his wife.

We only took Riley to this dog beach once because it was almost a three-hour drive from home. I think we spent a good two hours there and he had so much fun with all the other dogs he saw. I splashed around with him in the water and that was so much fun. On the way home, he did something he hardly ever did-he slept. On the way down, he stood for most of the trip.

A Day At The Beach

1

Several years ago, Larry said, "Riley, do you want to go bye-bye in the car?"

I got so excited because most times when we went somewhere in the car it was going to mean some fun times for me. I got up and started dancing and barking, showing my enthusiasm for our trip to a place where I could probably run and jump off the leash.

After I hopped in the back seat, we pulled out and Larry began to drive. I almost always stand when we are going on a ride because the longest drive we take is usually not more than a half an hour or so. I can't really be sure of how much time passed by, but it seemed like we were going a lot further than ever before. I said before that when I lived in Bensalem, the ride back to Hellertown was a little over an hour, and it seemed like that much time had passed when Larry pulled over, stopping at a convenience store.

Larry opened the door and I jumped out, wondering where we were. He walked me to a grassy area, where I peed for a long time. We walked back to the car and Larry put a small dish on the parking lot and put some water in it. I drank the whole amount because, even though it was cool in the car, with the air-conditioning on, it was getting pretty warm outside.

I hopped back in the car and we started off again. I still had no clue as to our destination and although I was getting tired of standing, I still did because I could see things passing by as the car was moving pretty fast.

Once again, Larry pulled into a parking lot and took me into a grassy area to go potty again. This time I peed and pooed. Larry picked up my bowel movement with a plastic bag, tied it in a knot and dropped it into a trash can. He gave me a little water and a little treat and then we hopped back in the car once again.

After driving for a pretty long time again, Peggy opened the car window and said, "Hey, Ri, can you smell the ocean, buddy?"

I had no idea what an ocean was but when we pulled into a parking lot and I got out, there was water for as far as I could see and a lot of sand. Larry left me off the leash and I took off, running through the sand and jumping into the water.

While Peggy set up their beach chairs and a blanket for me, along with a dish of water, I splashed around with a couple of other dogs and then Larry joined me in the water. It was so nice and warm and we swam and swam for a long time. I got a little tired so I headed back to the blanket and the fresh cool water. Peggy also gave me a couple of treats to keep my strength up.

I saw other dogs walking in the sand. A couple were chasing round disks that their peops were throwing through the air; the dogs would jump high and catch the disk, they called them Frisbees, in their mouths and then bring them back to their humans.

Larry brought a Frisbee, but for some reason, I wasn't too crazy about that game and when he threw the Frisbee, I just ignored it and ran back to the water, splashing and swimming with Peggy because she wanted to get wet to cool down before heading back to her chair and her book.

I don't remember how long we were at that beach, but after a long time of swimming and playing with other dogs, I got a little tired and laid down on the blanket again.

Larry looked at Peggy and said, "I think Ri is pooped out. He has been a very busy puppy for all this time. I think it's time to head to Ocean City and get some pizza."

At the mere mention of the word, I was up, wagging my tail, wondering where this Ocean City place was, and how soon would I be dining on some delicious pizza crusts. Maybe they'd give me more than crusts this time.

2

After going potty, we got back in the car and took a short drive. We crossed a long bridge and I saw all these white birds flying around just above the water. There were some back at the beach we were at, but none of them ever got close enough for me to sniff them and check them out completely, but it seemed like wherever there was a lot of water, these birds were there.

We drove into a little town and I saw lots of peops walking around in all manner of dress; some were wearing shorts and t-shirts, some in dresses and skirts, and some were wearing bathing suits, so I figured we must be near another beach.

Larry parked the car and opened my door, allowing me to jump out. We started walking, and I was so busy looking around at all the peops. Many of them were talking and laughing, carrying folding beach chairs and coolers. I could smell the ocean again and it made me so excited that I wondered if I was going to get to play in the water and on the sand again. Some peops stopped and petted me, after asking permission. They thought I was really handsome and some said cute.

We strolled up a wooden ramp to what was called the boardwalk, and my nostrils were just filling with the most amazing smells. I could pick out the scents of hamburgers and hot dogs, French fries, chocolate-although I can never have that because it could make me really sick, I've heard-soda, coffee, the unmistakable scent of frozen yogurt-I wondered if I would get a cup of that, too-onions, peppers, and some unrecognizable scents as well. Then I caught a good whiff of pizza.

Larry sat down on a bench, just off the main boardwalk. He talked to me to calm me and to keep my mind off all the good smells. "Riley, Peggy just went to get our pizza. Now you have to stay here and be really quiet and not cause any trouble with anyone walking by, because dogs aren't allowed on the boardwalk at this time of year." I was getting really hungry and anxious, so I whined a little to get his attention and all he did was grab my collar to keep me exactly where I was. I settled down a little bit and then two of those white birds landed real close to me and I wanted to get up and play with them, chasing them as far as I could. They got to within about two feet of me and then jumped up in the air and flew away. I looked up and saw lots of them and I just hoped that none of them would poop or pee on me. I heard that birds do that. I looked over at Larry and he was watching them closely too. He let go of my collar and gave me a little freedom of movement, but at that moment I saw Peggy come into view and she was carrying pizza.

She sat down next to Larry and they ate and pulled little pieces from the large slices and began feeding me. Gosh, it was so good and I was a very happy dog.

After we finished eating the pizza, we walked back to the car, hopped inside and started for home.

I think I was tired and actually took a nap, instead of standing up, not even concerned about the box of pizza in the trunk of the car, although I could smell it.

When we arrived at home, Larry took me for a short walk to go potty, even though we stopped again a couple of times on the way home.

He unleashed me and I bounded up the stairs as fast as I could and rushed right into the kitchen. I could smell pizza baking in the oven and a little later we all enjoyed more Mack and Manco pizza-the best pizza I have ever eaten.

This had been one of the best days of my life and I hoped we would do it again someday.

When I did the laundry, Riley would follow me from the laundry room to the bed, where I would place the wash to fold. Sometimes he would jump up on the bed and watch me. I threw a large handkerchief at him and it landed on his head. He just kept lying there, lifting his head long enough for me to take this picture. We had so much fun together.

Working by Larry

When I first met Riley in 2002 and then after I moved in with Peggy, I was a mailman. I always tried to only work an eight hour day, so that I could spend time with them and not be too tired. However, there were many times, especially in winter, that I took him out in the morning while it was till dark, and when I took him out after work, it was dark as well. There was never enough daylight on a winter's day to have fun with him and to spend quality time with Peggy before I was ready to crash for the night. The job was really beating me up as I grew older. My schedule was rotating days off. I would always be off on a Sunday, except for the one time I worked. It was such a boring day of delivering express mail and special deliveries and everything worked out in sixes. I worked six hours, delivered six pieces of mail and drove sixty-six miles.

So my off days would be Sunday and Monday the first week; Sunday and Tuesday the second week; then Sunday and Wednesday, Sunday and Thursday and then my long weekend would arrive and I would be off Friday, Saturday and Sunday. I think neither Peggy nor Riley liked that fact that I worked five out of six Saturdays since Peggy and I couldn't stay out late on Friday nights because I had to work on Saturday and Riley missed out on long walks on my work days.

I did get plenty of exercise for myself on my work days, especially being on the route I would retire from when I met Peggy and Riley. I had about 470 stops to make each day and all of my route was what was called park and loops. I would park the truck and deliver one to three blocks from each park point. I had twenty-two loops on this route, so there was a lot of work loading my satchel at each stop.

There were dogs on my route and I would take a moment or two to pet the safe ones and give them treats; however, there were those that were not safe and I tried to steer clear of them.

In the early part of my career, I ran into a couple of situations that, unfortunately were unavoidable.

One time I had just put a package between the storm door and the inside door because I heard barking and didn't want anyone to open the door. Well, a moment later, someone opened the door and a dog went for my hand. I quickly pulled away, but he got me with one tooth. I thought I was okay because it didn't draw blood, but after I walked away, I noticed the wound was bleeding. I called my supervisor and he sent someone out to finish my route and he took me to a nearby emergency center where I was treated. The dog was close to getting his rabies shot so I had to wait a period of a couple of days or so before I knew I would be okay. That was scary.

Another time I was crossing a lawn, paging mail when a small dog appeared in my vision. I saw him jump toward a spot just below my belt, so I dropped my hand to protect a certain area of my body. He tore into my hand and I needed to get a couple of stitches.

I think I was pretty lucky with having only two biting incidents in a 21 plus year career.

Again, back in the early part of my career, after my ninety-day probation was over, I was assigned to work in a nearby small town. On one route, every day I had to walk past a fence and I could hear the dog barking his fool head off, but I couldn't see him. One day after I delivered the mail, the dog stopped barking and I was concerned. I slowly turned around and there he was, with a ball in his mouth, wanting to play catch. We played catch for a little while and then I had to return to my route. I never had a problem with that dog.

Another time, I was subbing on a route and I was walking down the sidewalk when I saw a large German Shepard running toward me. I simply froze and hoped he wouldn't attack me. He stopped right in front up me and then jumped up, throwing his legs over my shoulders, licking my face like crazy. He got down and followed me the rest of the loop and when I got back to my truck, which was parked just a little past his house, he sat down and waited until I opened the door and got a treat for him. Apparently the regular carrier gave him treats all the time and he figured I would too.

The most amazing incident occurred about a year after I became a mailman. I parked on the street and had to walk up a bunch of concrete steps and a fairly long pavement to get to the house. The dog, a black and white mixed mongrel would almost always be laying in the yard waiting for me. I'd bend down and pet him and the dog would actually smile. One day, after I put the mail in the mailbox and walked toward my jeep, having left the door open, the dog was sitting on the seat with his paws over the steering wheel, smiling and shaking his head back and forth. I never saw anything like that before or ever again and he never did that again, even though I gave him many opportunities.

After I moved in with Peggy, and I came home from work, Riley would smell lots of dog smells on me and I think his feelings were hurt until I'd take him out and then give him treats and play with him a little when we came back inside.

When I retired and started working part time, I wouldn't have to leave the house until after 9 AM and I would be back by 3:30. Riley and I had plenty of time for walking and talking during this period of time, even though I was working five days a week.

About a year later, I took a new job and I only worked Monday through Wednesday leaving plenty of time to take care of him.

The final two and a half months of his life, I worked Monday, Tuesday and Wednesday and then I had seven days off. Then I worked Thursday and Friday, off the weekend and began my schedule again. I spent a lot of time with Riley during this time period, but he wasn't enjoying the things we used to do together. I'd take him out for fifteen to twenty minutes; longer as his time grew shorter, and it was a struggle for him to even go to the bathroom, yet he still enjoyed the time we spent together.

I still miss seeing him when I come home from work.

The End
Our Final Five Days With Riley

January 31st, 2015

Peggy and I were on the way home from a night of great food, fun and music with friends. She had been talking to several friends about when they had to put their dogs down and she told me she was pretty sure that Riley had dog dementia.

I think I was in denial, even though I could see the complications my best four-legged friend was having. For quite some time, his arthritic hips were giving him great difficulty laying down and then getting back up again. I marveled at his resilience, figuring out how to work his legs in such a manner that he could settle down into sometimes uncomfortable positions, though he complained little. Getting up he would work his front paws into a position that he was able to shift his body weight and stand up.

Over the last few months, or more, it's hard to recall, his back began to arch until he had somewhat of a hump back. Yet, he just kept going, still enjoying his walks, even though I had to shorten them considerably. Basically, I'd take him out long enough to do his business and then we'd come back into the house. Walking the equivalent of perhaps six blocks sometimes took us nearly twenty minutes to complete.

For some time, he has not been able to go up and down the stairs on his own, and I would have to go down backwards and guide him down the stairs. A few days ago, I fell and hurt my back, having to take two days off from work, but I would do anything to keep Riley going. In my selfishness, I'm sure I have kept him alive because I didn't want to lose him. He has been my buddy for nearly twelve and a half of his just over fourteen years. I have pretty much been his fulltime caretaker for about a year and a half, because he couldn't keep his footing on the hardwood floors at Sean's house. Sean asked if I would like the job of being Riley's custodian for the remainder of his life. Although I did not want a fulltime dog, I loved that brown and white, 35 pound Springer-Lab so very much.

We both knew that we would have to have Riley put to sleep in the very near future. It would be one of the hardest decisions I'd ever make.

February 1st, 2015

As usual, I woke up, had a cup of coffee and then woke Riley. We needed to go out so he could go potty. The cold mornings were not good for either of us, so on those days, I tried to hurry him along, and if I was off, I'd wind up taking him out two or three times until he did his business. For several weeks he'd lose his bowels or urinate in the house and it was getting me frustrated. I was feeling that I wasn't taking care of him as well as I could.

We came back inside and he fell asleep, something he has been doing more often and for longer periods of time than ever.

I went to church and prayed that Riley could be better, but God and I both knew that wouldn't happen. I told a friend that we would probably have to put him down before the following weekend and I just couldn't stop crying. My selfishness was coming out in the form of tears that just didn't want to quit. I was really having a tough time dealing with the fact that his quality of life was mostly gone. He never played with his toys anymore, but he still had a wonderful appetite and that made me feel that perhaps he could still have a longer life. I was just fooling myself.

February 2nd, 2015

Before going to work, I like to watch a little TV and check out my email and see what is happening on Facebook.

Riley was a little restless and he was wandering around what I call the Riley highway. He walks between the sofa and the coffee table, heads toward the top of the stairs, looks out the balcony door and then he looks down the steps. He turns around and walks past the TV, hooks a left and stops at his bowl for a couple of sips of water and a few bites of food. Then he turns to his right, circles the dining room table and heads back to walk the route again.;

We have a gate because on Trick or Treat night last year, I was outside handing candy to the kids. I looked toward the door and saw Riley standing inside the door. He had come down the stairs by himself, not falling, but he did it again a few times after that, so after Christmas I put up a child's gate. I had forgotten to lock it after we came back from our walk. After he looked down the stairs, I saw him go. He fell to the first landing and hit his head on an antique school desk. Fortunately he was okay, but I went to the bedroom and told Peg that now I truly believed I needed to let go. I never would want to see Riley in pain from breaking a bone. I thought I was pretty secure in my decision, but old man selfishness always gets in the way, doesn't it?

After Peg came home from work, we had dinner and discussed what we should do. We both agreed that Friday night would probably be a good time to have someone come in and administer the meds that would have Riley gently and quickly pass, with no pain. Peg told me that she wanted to get him a whole slice of pizza and make him happy. Pizza and McDonald's French fries were his two favorite people foods. Of course, my puppy never turned any people food away. I thought that to be a very good idea and it would be fun to see him enjoy something before he had to go. I still have trouble saying the word 'die' because death seems so final.

Peggy made the call but there was no answer, so she left a message. I was starting to accept the fact that soon Riley would be gone, leaving me with so many good memories, but it still was hard to keep my composure whenever I talked about his impending death to anyone.

I had been sleeping on the sofa, keeping him company and during the night I heard him wandering around. When he decided to lay down again, he was groaning and crying because I imagine his pain was becoming more present. It hurt me so bad, that I would be so self-centered, wanting to keep him alive, even though I knew he was having more pain.

February 3rd, 2015

I told my co-workers that we would probably put Riley to sleep on Friday evening, so we wouldn't have to think about him while trying to do our jobs all day the following day. I thought that would probably be easier for me to handle-once again self-centered Larry was going to have things made a little easier for himself.

That was not to be because Peggy called me and went over the expense and the additional cost of having a weekend euthanasia performed. We agreed that we would take Riley to the vet on Wednesday. I was a mess for the rest of the day. Now it was nearly final. Riley would be gone in less than thirty hours. This was confirmed after I came home from work and agreed that we had to end his suffering.

I took Ri out for a short walk and when I came back, Peg had called the vet and we were given a 6 PM time slot.

I've been giving him a bunch of treats and he napped a little, way less than normal. I had a talk with him about what I hoped dog heaven would be like and that he would probably see his puppy friends who have gone before. For some time Riley has been the senior dog of our condo community and when he is gone, I don't know who will take that title.

He spent most of the evening wandering around, seemingly very confused. I was laying on the sofa, trying to get a little rest because I figured that I wouldn't get much sleep tonight.

Peggy came home about 10:30 and we talked a little and she petted Riley a lot. She went to bed and I tried to get to sleep as I heard him walking around in the darkness. Soon, I didn't hear him anymore, so I thought he went to sleep. I told her he had two Frosty Paws instead of one.

Peggy called my name and then told me that Riley was stuck between the seat and base of my computer chair. I started in, seeing the fear in his eyes, but I was still in the hallway when he worked himself free. He had been getting stuck in so many different places. He'd work his way behind my chair, knock over the lamp and try to come back out by going under the end table. He broke the leg on one occasion, so I will have to re-glue it sometime this weekend. He tried to get through the baby's walker and got stuck in there. He once got stuck under a dining room chair. He had somehow climbed over the leg braces on one side and when he tried to come out the other side, he got wedged and I had to work with him to get him out of that spot.

Peg came out to the living room a few minutes later. I was sitting on the sofa watching Ri try to get into a position to lie down. He would sometimes circle for several minutes, groaning and grunting, until he was finally in a comfortable position in which he could rock back and forth and finally lay down. I told Peg to stay where she was, assuming, correctly, that Riley would fall asleep in a few minutes.

February 4th, 2015

I finally fell asleep sometime after looking at my watch, seeing it was 12:34 AM. Riley now only had less than 18 hours before our appointment at the vet at 6 PM.

I woke up several times during the night, and he was sleeping comfortably. That made me feel good, because I had a feeling, wrong this time, thankfully, that he would be up and down throughout the night.

I woke up at 3:00 AM and went to the bathroom. I took my diabetes meds and then laid down for about forty minutes. I showered, dressed, tested my blood and then had a cup of coffee and a banana. I would test my blood again around 6 AM and then have my second cup of coffee.

When I was in the bathroom, I head Riley jingle his dog license, so I knew he was up. I hoped I wouldn't find anything on the floor before taking him out, but he had already peed. He had been doing this anywhere between three and seven days a week for several weeks, sometimes a couple of times a day. I took him out and he peed again, but he didn't poop. Chances are when I come home from work, there will be a mess on the floor.

I gave him a dish of food and water. He ate a little bit and drank some water. Now he is sleeping on the floor in front of my chair. If he doesn't wake up before I leave for work, I'll let him sleep.

It's now 5:10 AM and my buddy will be gone in a little over thirteen hours. I will be sad for a long time to come. Mornings and evenings will be the hardest times because those are the times I would interact with Riley the most, especially having one-sided conversations with him.

When I arrived home from work, Riley was just waking up. He needed help to stand, and I thought how I would never have the opportunity to help him out again because in a little over two hours he would be gone, in a better place, young, strong, and happy once again.

I took him for his final potty walk but I made a call to one friend, who was one of the best friends Riley had. She came out and comforted me, petted Ri, and we both had a good cry before I took him back home.

Peggy came home with a slice of pizza for our good little boy, but before he was to eat his treat, she called Sean and the three of them spent some face time.

Riley got his slice of pizza and gobbled it down. He smiled a lot. I gave him a Frosty Paw and Peg took pictures of him eating it. He was a happy dog at this moment.

Riley is enjoying his final Frosty Paw. I posted this picture on my Facebook page after returning from the vet. My daughter-in-law posted "I don't know where Riley is, but I am sure the streets are lined with Frosty Paws." I imagine he is in a field on the other side of the Rainbow Bridge playing with his dog friends, chasing moths, squirrels and rabbits.

When we arrived at the animal hospital, I walked Riley inside. In the past, he used to go crazy, running around and barking, clearly not wanting to be here. Now, he just strolled in and stood still while we waited for service. They wanted to weigh him, so I led him to the scale and lifted him on. He stood perfectly still, something that never happened before. He used to try to jump off and it was difficult getting a good weight. The last time he had been on that scale was about a year ago. He weighed about 35 pounds at that visit-now he weighed 30.5.

We took him into a room where a doggie bed was on the floor. I helped him to lie down and just kept petting him for a while. Peggy also comforted him and we petted him for a few minutes before a tech came in to take him to get a catheter put in his leg. He offered no resistance and I guess I finally figured out that he was probably so confused, that nothing bothered him. He laid back down and we petted him and talked to him for a few minutes before the vet came in with several syringes.

She told us she was going to give him a sedative to relax him and after she did, I could feel his muscles soften; even his fur felt softer to me. He laid his head down and then we told her to administer the final medicine that would end his life. She did and about two minutes later, at 6:51 PM, Riley was gone. The vet left the room.

Peg and I cried so hard for a few minutes. I kissed him on the top of the head and told him I loved him. I had to get out of there and give Peg a little time with our little boy.

We went to get a bite to eat and two drinks, talking about the life of Riley.

When we entered our condo, it just felt so cold and empty without him.

Riley, I will miss you until we meet again someday. You were the best puppy ever and no other dog could ever replace you. You will be my final dog, buddy.

Rest in peace, Riley.

Peggy and Riley on one of our many walks at Lehigh.

Peggy And Riley

Our Riley was the sweetest, cutest dog ever. He looked like a cartoon character with his floppy ears, freckles, and long white streak on his soft beautiful dark brown fur. However, this is not what I saw the first time we met. Prior to meeting Riley, my son wanted an adorable, lively, red cocker spaniel. He was living in the basement of a kennel and desperately wanted a new home. On our way to pick him up, Sean wanted to check another pet store. I was not concerned because I knew he would never find any puppy cuter than "Red." Well, within 10 minutes, I was proven wrong. Sean found Riley who was sitting in his crate looking very sad. He had injured his mouth on the steel crate. Sean asked if he could be placed on the floor. Riley went immediately to Sean and put his head on Sean's leg. They both looked so happy. I had to walk away so Sean did not see my tears. All of I could think about was "Red" all alone in the basement and waiting for us to come and rescue him.

A few minutes later, Sean came and said he had to have Riley. So off we went with Riley sitting on Sean's lap just staring at me. I was convinced he knew I did not want him. A snow storm was on the way and we had to get canned food for him due to his injury. We were able to get everything and get settled in the house before driving conditions became hazardous.

A few hours later, Riley began to have diarrhea and I had to follow him all over the house trying to keep a towel under him. I had recently purchased a condo with white carpeting and now it was being ruined by a puppy I did not want. He was also chewing all the furniture and my shoes. I had to 'puppy proof' the house quickly. Over the next few hours, Riley's diarrhea became worse and we had to contact a vet. They told us we had to stop feeding him the canned food and get him a special brand of dry food.

In the meantime, we are in the midst of snow storm and did not know where to purchase the food. We called several places and discovered that a store less than a mile away carried this brand of food. I was able to get there and Riley was able to try some that evening. Finally, the diarrhea stopped and he settled down for the evening. I began to feel sorry for him and picked him up and put him on my bed.

After a few minutes, he came over and laid his head on my leg. As I petted him, I began to feel closer to him. Within a few days, we were buddies. Then the fun began as he chewed my shoes and several pieces of furniture. He was active and loved to get into trouble but I still loved him and miss him every day.

I will never forget how excited he was every time anyone came into the house. He loved to jump and give everyone a kiss. He was only about 35 lbs. but he did frighten some little ones. He loved to run in the field, he enjoyed the neighborhood dogs, his swim in the creek, and his long walks.

Sean and Riley on Christmas, 2013.

Sean And Riley

Riley was my buddy He loved to follow me everywhere. He loved to eat and would go crazy when he smelled pizza and French fries. I can still see him sitting on the floor, staring at me and hoping I would give him a bite. He also loved to run and jump. Every evening I would take him out to the dog park and let him run. He never liked to play fetch but he was always ready to run with me or his dog friends. He was the fastest and could certainly jump the highest. I will always smile when I think of Riley and he will always be my best buddy.

ABOUT THE AUTHOR

Larry Deibert has written seven novels; 95 Bravo-published by www.writers-exchange in 2004;Requiem For A Vampire-published by Mundania Press in 2007; Combat Boots dainty feet-Finding Love in Vietnam (a rewrite of 95 Bravo), published by www.lulu.com in 2009; The Christmas City Vampire, published originally by Bradley Publishings in 2012 and then released by the author on www.createspace.com in 2013; The Other Side Of The Ridge-Gettysburg, June 27th 2013 to July 2nd, 1863, published in 2013 by www.writers-exchange.com; Fathoms-A Novel Of The Paranormal, published by www.createspace.com in 2014; From Darkness To Light, published by www.createspace.com in 2014.

He is a Vietnam veteran and is the past president of the Lehigh Northampton Vietnam Veterans Memorial

He retired from the U.S. Postal Service in 2008 after working as a letter carrier for over 21 years.

Larry and his wife, Peggy, live in Hellertown, Pa., where he enjoys reading and writing. He has two grown children, Laura and Matthew.

In their spare time Larry and Peggy love to travel to the beaches on the East Coast. They have gone on two cruises and in 2003 had a dream trip to England and Scotland. In Scotland, Larry was thrilled to play golf at the St. Andrews complex.

He is currently working on several projects. Family is a novel about a 'family' of immortals spanning 226 years He is writing his first werewolf novel, Werewolves In The Christmas City. Larry is also working on Family Book 2. Several novels, novellas and short stories are in various stages of completion.

Larry L. Deibert and Riley

I hope you enjoyed reading this book about a most amazing, wonderful dog. I was blessed to have him for so long.

Made in the USA
Middletown, DE
26 March 2019